ABOVE: *Fitting the shoe — the final stage of nailing the shoe on to the hoof.*
COVER: *'Shoeing the Bay Mare' by Landseer, from a coloured print.*

OLD HORSESHOES

Ivan G. Sparkes

Shire Publications Ltd

CONTENTS

Copyright ©1976 by Ivan G. Sparkes. Shire Album No. 19. ISBN 0 85263 348 3. First published 1976, reprinted 1979 and 1983.

Printed in Great Britain by City Print (Milton Keynes) Ltd, Denbigh Hall, Bletchley, Bucks.

View of the ornamental horseshoes in Oakham Castle. Taking pride of place is the shoe presented by the Prince Regent in 1814, surmounted by three feathers.

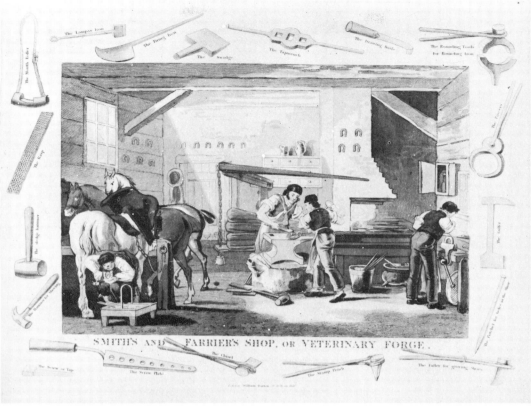

The blacksmith's or farrier's shop of the early nineteenth century. Engraving by William Darton of London.

ROMAN AND ROMANO-BRITISH
SHOES AND HIPPO-SANDALS

In its natural state the horny casing of the foot of a horse is quite sufficient to meet the demands made upon it, but, when domestication took place, working the animal continuously on hard ground and paved road caused the horny casing to wear away rapidly or break.

The use of horseshoes to prevent this damage, or to help the horse when it occurred, seems to date back to Roman times when they were attached to the horse's foot by cords or leather straps on special occasions. The nailed shoe may possibly have originated among the Celts of north-western Europe.

One of the problems which hinder research into the use of the shoe in these early periods is the absence of examples or good archaeological evidence for their former use. Michael Cuddeford, in a recent article, points to the fact that when a Roman cavalry fort on Hadrian's Wall was excavated, no shoes with nail-holes were discovered, although other iron objects had survived the ravages of time. Of course it is also probable that auxiliary cavalry on the wall used local hill ponies whose feet would not have needed protection during forays over rough ground.

Sometimes a kind of slipper made of Spanish broom or leather was used to protect horses' hoofs when travelling on rough ground. Later a thin plate of metal tied to the horse's foot by means of leather straps gave more substantial protection. It was known to the Romans as a *solea ferrea* and archaeologists today call it a 'hippo-sandal'.

George Fleming, in his treatise on the horseshoe (1869), divides hippo-sandals into three main types:

1. An oval or oblong plate of iron, with a circular opening in the centre. Two or four clips rise from its sides terminating in rings or hooks which held the leather thong or strap used to tie the shoe to the hoof.
2. A similar plate to that used in (1), but with a long spur or heel at the back terminating in a hook. It has another spur at the front.
3. A similar plate with a back hook, but no front spur. The two front side-clips have been extended up and forward to meet and be joined together as a hoop under which the hoof was fitted.

The use of these hippo-sandals has been the subject of much controversy over the years, as they are quite bulky, about 5½ inches long and 3¼ inches wide with iron clips rising to 5 inches. One specimen at Hull Museum weighed 23¼ ounces. Mortimer Wheeler stated that 'there is little doubt that these objects were in fact a form of readily adjustable and removable shoe in use in a time when horses were doubtless worked frequently without shoes at all'. Michael Cuddeford considers them a 'get-you-home' device to be used if the horse went lame, or for use as a hobble to stop horses from wandering too far from home. However, I am reminded by John Anstee that incontrovertible evidence for their use on horses has been found at a site on Rome's Persian frontier. Here the skeleton of a horse was excavated with hippo-sandals on all four feet, which confirms their use in historical times.

The literary evidence regarding early horseshoes is most interesting. Catullus (84–54 BC) criticises the state of mind of his contemporaries in a poem, advising them to 'leave your sluggish mind sunk in thick mire, as the mule his iron shoe in the tenacious bog'. This reference to iron for shoes is confirmed by much later writers. Vegetius Renatus, writing in AD *c.* 383–450, tells the horse-owner that 'you shall shoe his feet that are sound with an iron patten or sandal'. Other metals were also used. Suetonius tells us that Nero (AD 37–68) never travelled unless accompanied by a thousand four-wheeled chariots, drawn by mules whose feet were shod with silver, and the wife of Nero is reputed to have ordered that her favourite mules be shod in gold. In this context I suspect that a decorative upper shoe or covering was used, and not an actual protective shoe as we would consider it.

The first specific reference to nailed horseshoes is probably that quoted in the *Tactica* of the Emperor Leo VI (AD 886–911) where, among a list of items essential to the cavalryman, are included 'lunar or crescent-shaped iron shoes and their nails'. It is certain that nailed shoes were in use as early as the fifth century AD, and some writers postulate their existence within iron-age communities, with the terms 'Romano-British' and 'Celtic' shoes frequently applied to them. Unfortunately there is no prominent change of style or of detail which allows us to identify these early shoes and separate them from those of the early Norman period, nor does archaeological evidence place them firmly in a chronological sequence. Due to these factors, I have found it convenient to group the shoes in this book into types with common physical features, rather than to try to fit them into hard and fast time periods.

This sketch shows the way in which the hippo-sandal was attached to the horse's hoof.

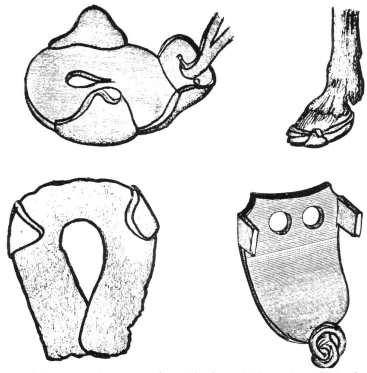

The hippo-sandal type one has two or four side-clips which terminate in hooks or rings and a rear clip or ring. The top left illustration shows the sandal with the leather strap in position; when the hoof is inserted, the strap slips under the iron hoops each side and is fastened at the rear. The lower left sandal, discovered at Remennecourt, bears a strong resemblance to a medieval shoe, while the lower right sandal has no hooks on the sides, nor do the clips bend over to fit the shape of the hoof. Therefore some other method of lacing the leather strap through the centre holes must have been used.

The hippo-sandal with an advanced model of type one, showing a more pronounced 'heel' to the rear spur, and the rings curved over more to the centre of the sandal. The top right sandal (discovered in 1854–5 at Dalheim) and the centre right sandal show the side-clips almost joined together, there being just sufficient room to lace a leather thong through the hooks. The sandals top left (Cluny Museum) and lower centre, are similar but include the clips terminating in rings instead of hooks.

LEFT: *A silver coin of Tarentum, the ancient name for Taranto in Italy. The coin is in the British Museum and dated as c. 300 BC. The rider on the back of the horse appears to be soothing it to allow the other figure to crouch beside it to remove or replace a shoe or sandal. As no tools are present, it is possible that a temporary shoe or hippo-sandal is involved.*

A hippo-sandal from Hull Museum's collection.

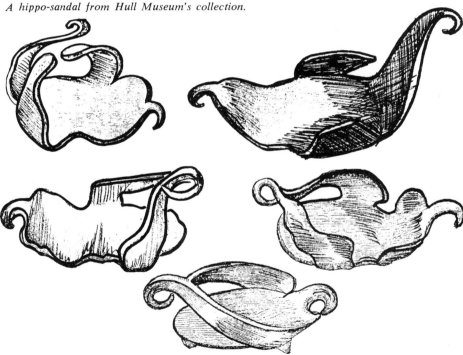

Hippo-sandal type two (top left and right), showing the highly extended rear spur, now rising to five inches, and the small spur at the front to give extra security when threading the leather strap or thong. The remaining three illustrate type three, probably the final development. The front spur has been removed, the rear spur reduced and the side-clips are now joined across the sole to form a hoop into which the hoof will fit. The centre right sandal, excavated in London, shows the typical linking of the elongated side pieces, while the lower sandal, from near Stuttgart, shows two of the three studs or calks which were riveted into the sole plate on the road side of the sandal. The clips, where they join, form into a curled hook or eyelet through which the leather strap can be drawn.

Good example of wavy-rim shoe, probably early Saxon or Celtic with six holes and slight calkin on heels. Shows oval depression which has distorted the shoe ($3\frac{1}{2}$ oz).

Saxon wavy-rim shoe with more precisely punched nail-holes and calkin on only one branch, c. 9th-10th century (4 oz).

Saxon wavy-rim shoe, probably 9th-10th century, still using the six round nail-holes but the depression is now punched with oblong shape and calkins turned over (5 oz).

Norman shoe, 11th century, with six square nail-holes and the wavy outline showing transition to the smooth rim (4 oz).

Norman shoe, 11th-12th century, calkins on both branches, but rather worn (5 oz).

Late Norman shoe, 13th century, which has almost lost its wavy rim, and the inner rim has become more regular; a larger shoe (7 oz).

Well-preserved late Norman shoe, thirteenth century, with well-formed calkins, deep clean countersunk punching and large oblong nail-holes (7 oz).

THE WAVY-RIMMED HORSESHOE

These early shoes are believed to be a development of the metal plate which was the basis of the hippo-sandal. At first the hole was cut in the centre of the plate; this lightened the shoe and gave the horse a better foothold. In time the circular rim which remained was opened up at the heel, and the excess overlap of the plate beyond the contour of the hoof was reduced until something approaching our present conception of a shoe developed. This shoe was much narrower in section than formerly and followed the basic shape of the horse's hoof, so it could be made from a metal strip or bar instead of the larger iron plates used in Roman times.

It seems probable that the use of shoes was not common until the later Saxon period, when the horses were more frequently shod, a fact which can be assumed from several references in the Domesday book (AD 1086). At Hereford in the time of Edward the Confessor 'there were six smiths in the city; each of them rendered one penny from his forge and each of them made 120 shoes of the King's iron, and each of them was given three pence on that account, according to the custom'.

The shoe of this period was not large, probably averaging 4 by 4 inches, and the significant feature of the type group is the wavy outer rim, prominent on all examples from the earliest to those dating to the thirteenth century. This bulging at the rim near the nail-holes arose from the method of production and was not a matter of contrived design. The iron bar used was about half to three quarters of an inch wide and was heated and bent, then three large oval depressions were hot-punched about two thirds of the way through the thickness of the iron on each branch; circular holes for the nails were then punched inside them, right through the metal. The narrow band of iron could not take this drastic treatment without distortion and consequently bulged outwards around the holes, giving the familiar serpentine effect.

The nails associated with the shoes of pre-Norman date were made with a 'fiddle key' shaped top. Although the nail-holes sat within the countersunk depressions, the nail-heads still protruded by almost half their length, so that the horse actually walked on them and the folded-over calkins.

The hoof surface of the shoe was flat, but the underside or road surface (often called the wearing surface) was rounded, and the calkins, which are the thickened sections at the heel of each branch of the shoe, were made by bending down and folding back the end of each branch. Calkins acted as a steadying factor in stopping the shoe from slipping on muddy or smooth hard ground. Gordon Ward hints that early shoes were used chiefly as a non-slip device, rather than the more acceptable idea of protection for the hoof from wear or damage.

As the shoe developed during the Norman period, the nail-holes became square in shape and their number increased from the usual six per shoe of the early iron-age or Celtic shoe to seven or eight holes per shoe by the mid thirteenth century. The nail in use changed also, and the T-shaped, square-sectioned nail, which probably came over from the Continent with the invaders, was adopted.

Toe-clips are seldom noted in these earlier shoes, and the heels were wide apart with the shape of the shoe almost as long as it was wide. With the later Saxon and early Norman shoes, the branches tend to be extended, creating a shoe which is fractionally longer than its width. In the mid Norman period, this is about $4\frac{1}{2}$ by $3\frac{3}{4}$ inches, and the branches, which taper towards the heel, are brought closer together.

It was the practice of both Saxons and Normans to shoe the forefeet only and by the medieval period warhorses were taught to fight with their shod front feet, and in this context they may be regarded as weapons.

The wavy rim, which was so noticeable up to the eleventh and twelfth centuries, becomes less prominent in the thirteenth century, until with the medieval shoe of the fourteenth century it virtually disappears.

Characteristics of the wavy-rimmed shoe
Early period (up to the eleventh century)
1. Wavy outline.
2. Six round nail-holes within oval depressions.
3. Size: length roughly equal to width, i.e. 4 by 4 inches.
4. Weight: $3\frac{1}{2}$–5 ounces.
5. Width of iron: $\frac{1}{2}$-$\frac{3}{4}$ inch.
6. Rounded lower surface, a flat upper.
7. Wide open heels which taper.
8. Turned-over calkins.
9. Fiddle-headed nails.

Later period (eleventh to fourteenth centuries)
1. Wavy outline disappearing later in the thirteenth century.
2. Six round nail-holes changing to seven and then eight and becoming square in shape.
3. Fiddle-headed nails replaced by T-shaped square-sectioned nails.
4. Size: becoming slightly longer than their width, i.e. $4\frac{1}{2}$ by $3\frac{3}{4}$ inches.
5. Weight: 4–7 ounces.
6. Heels drawn together, branches slightly longer.

LEFT: *Guildhall shoe, late fourteenth century to early fifteenth century, with six square nail-holes and the remains of a T-shaped nail in one hole ($4\frac{3}{4}$ by $4\frac{1}{2}$ inches, $8\frac{1}{2}$ oz). Draught-horse shoe with typical arched frog of the period.* RIGHT: *Guildhall shoe c. 1400 with seven or eight holes, calkin on one branch ($5\frac{1}{2}$ by $4\frac{1}{2}$ inches, 8 oz).*

GUILDHALL AND DOVE SHOES

The state of the roads and the type of horse in use are critical factors in the development of the shoe. In the early Norman period the great importance placed on shoeing becomes apparent from the increasing number of instances where shoes or horse-shoeing itself formed part of an annual tax or tribute. Henry de Averyng held the manor of Mórton in Essex of the King by finding a man with a horse and four horseshoes 'as often as it may happen that our Lord the King should go with his army into Wales'. In 1235 Walter le Brun was also granted a piece of land in the Strand, on which to build a forge, but he had to render annually to the Exchequer as quit-rent six shoes and their nails.

Also noticeable is the way certain districts or cities became well-known centres for the making of shoes and nails. Gloucester, in the Domesday Book, paid annually to the King some thirty-six dacras of iron and one hundred

bars of iron fit for the manufacture of nails for the navy. The 'dacras' mentioned in the reference is a measure which in 1195, as a dacrum, was twenty shoes. This local industry is further commemorated on a medieval seal of the city, granted by Edward III and renewed by Richard III. On it the horseshoe assumes heraldic significance and, when the county of Gloucestershire was granted arms in 1935, the new shield incorporated three shoes. The extent of the trade becomes apparent when it is realised that in the reign of Richard I, over fifty thousand shoes were made for use on the Crusades, without counting those made for the home market.

To meet the requirements of the mounted chivalry (when the weight of the armour and rider in the fifteenth century amounted to 30 stone) heavier horses were imported from the Continent. On one occasion during the reign of King John, there is a record of one hundred stallions of large stature being imported from Flanders. This hints at the origin of the comment about Anne of Cleves, Henry VIII's wife, as being the 'Flanders Mare'. As domestic and military horses grew in size, so the size of the shoes changed, with the wavy-rimmed type disappearing by *c.* 1300. Some early examples of the fullered shoe, possibly from the Flemish and Burgundian farriers, are believed to date to the later years of this period.

At this point (about 1350–1400) the development of the English horseshoe splits into two main streams. It should be borne in mind that there is a distinction between the saddle or hackney horse and the draught horse and heavy mule, and it follows that some differences will exist in the shoes made for them. The wavy-rimmed shoe, now with its outer edge smoothed out, but retaining its basic shape and light weight, became the type used on saddle or riding horses, while the heavier Flemish or Burgundian type, which came across with the imported stallions of the thirteenth and fourteenth centuries, formed the pattern for the shoe of the draught horse.

The saddle-horse shoe is an intermediate type, represented by the later models of the 'Guildhall' shoe, and later still by the 'Dove' shoe. This started off as a simple 6-ounce shoe with a curved outer and arched inner shape, frequently with one calkin and with three square holes for nails on each branch, sometimes with four holes on one side and three on the other. The new inner arched shaped is interesting, and an analogy between it and the Early English style of arch in use in churches at the time has been commented upon. This type of shoe has been dated by Gordon Ward as *c.* 1250, and as it appears on the city of Gloucester seal of 1398, we can assume its use goes up to that date. A similar shoe for the saddle horse, but one with a slightly slimmer shape and having narrower branches, has been called the 'Dove' shoe (from its discovery in the river Dove in Staffordshire) and it can be accurately dated at 1322. It is about $4\frac{1}{2}$ by $4\frac{1}{2}$ inches and has one calkin and three nailholes on each branch. In shape it is more symmetrical and is much nearer to what we accept as the traditional horseshoe.

The shoe of the draught horse is again of the 'Guildhall' type, having the arched inner shape and similarity to the shoes modelled on the later Gloucester shield of *c.* 1483. Also characteristic of the 'Guildhall' type is

LEFT: *Seal of Ralph, farrier to the bishopric of Durham. The seal shows a heavy horseshoe with six square holes and two nails of the spiked or frost variety.* RIGHT: *Sixteenth-century Guildhall-type shoe with heavy calkins, dated 1573, which was nailed to the church door of Sainte-Saturnin.*

ABOVE: *Early Guildhall shoe with six nail-holes, probably 1250-70; note the two square-headed nails in one hole, hammered over (4⅛ by 4 inches, 7 oz).*

ABOVE: *Guildhall shoe with six well-formed nail-holes, fifteenth century, for a saddle horse and possibly a surgical shoe as there are no nail-holes in the narrow inner branch (4¾ by 3⅞ inches, 7 oz).*

BELOW: *Guildhall draught-horse shoe, 1400-50 (5½ by 4¾ inches, 11 oz).*

BELOW: *Guildhall transitional shoe, 1500-50, with seven nail-holes and the beginning of the keyhole shape (5½ by 4⅝ inches, 10 oz).*

Two shoes made by Joe Price, a Gloucestershire blacksmith, in the style of shoes illustrated in books or on seals, etc: (left) from the fifteenth–century arms of the city of Gloucester; (right) from an early sixteenth-century vellum roll in the College of Arms showing Henry VIII's horse at a tournament of 1511.

the shoe illustrated in 1565 in *The four chiefest offices belonging to horsemanship* by Master Blundevil of Norfolk. Blundevil writes at length about the drawbacks of country smiths, and suggests that the shoe should be made of spruce or Spanish iron, the calkins more substantial and the square-headed nails fitted to protrude no more than 'the breadth of the back of a knife' below the level of the shoe.

One dating feature in the medieval or 'Guildhall' period is the introduction of what Gordon Ward calls the 'spiked nail', which is also commonly known as the 'frosty nail' from its use in icy weather to help steady the horse. Some research done on this feature and on the seals used on dated documents has shown the spiked nail to have been in use between 1254 and 1301. This gives rise to the belief that it superseded the square-headed or T-shaped nail in lighter Guildhall shoes about the middle of the fourteenth century, and in the heavier Guildhall draught shoe somewhat later. This heavier shoe was therefore in use from

the late fifteenth century up to and possibly well into the seventeenth century, while the lighter saddle shoe covered the period from the fourteenth to the seventeenth century with considerable regional variations. It was these differences which almost led to the capture of Charles II after the battle of Worcester. When Charles arrived at Lyme Regis, a smith was called in to attend to the horses; suddenly he turned to Charles and asked: 'What manner of man are you whose horse has been shod in three different counties, and one of them Worcester?'

Characteristics of the Guildhall shoe

1. Round outer edge, arched inner edge, the point of the arch disappears by the early sixteenth century.
2. Width of iron at the toe in the heavy draught shoes can be up to 2–2½ inches.
3. Long branches with heels inclined together.

ABOVE: *Dove shoe, early fourteenth century, a saddle shoe, the calkins worn or absent, rather roughly forged (4⅞ by 4⅜ inches, 9 oz).*

BELOW: *Dove shoe, mid fourteenth century, six nail-holes and one T-shaped nail still in position. Calkin on one branch (4¾ by 4½ inches, 6 oz).*

ABOVE: *Dove shoe, late thirteenth century, still with six square nail-holes and with wedge-shaped calkin on one branch (5 oz).*

BELOW: *Gloucester city arms of the fifteenth century.*

4. Calkins are absent on heavy draught shoes of the later period; sixteenth-century examples often have thick turned-down calkins. The lighter saddle shoe usually has one calkin.
5. Square nail-holes, with chisel-edge nails on draught-horse shoes; the square or chisel-edge nail changed to the spiked nail with the saddle-horse shoe of about 1300.
6. Shoes have become flatter and broader than those of the earlier periods.
7. Weight and size: draught shoe 5 by 4½ inches, 12–18 ounces; saddle shoe 4¼ by 4½ inches, 4–7 ounces.

Characteristics of the Dove shoe
1. Round outer and inner shape, no bulges.
2. One calkin.
3. Usually three nail-holes on one branch and four on the other.
4. Weight and size: 4 by 4 inches, 5–7 ounces.

15

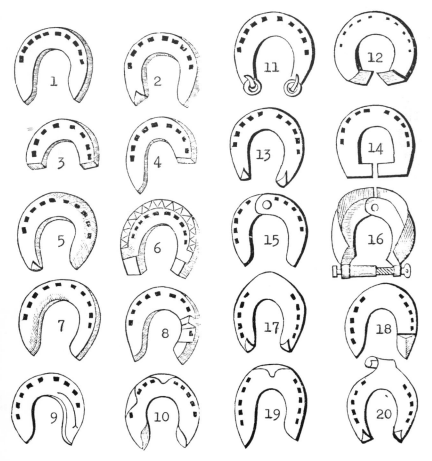

Types of horseshoe used on the Continent (1564), illustrated in a treatise by Caesar Fiaschi and reprinted by George Fleming (1869): 1. Fore shoe without calkins; 2. Shoe with calkin on one side; 3. Lunette or 'half' shoe; 4. Three-quarter shoe; 5. Bevelled shoe with calkin on one branch and the other thickened; 6. Shoe with sciettes or projecting toothed border, thickened into a solid calkin at heels; 7. Thick-sided shoe, rounded towards the inner rim; 8. Shoe with buttons or raised catches on the inner branch, and thickened into a solid calkin on same side; 9. Shoe with inside heel and quarter much thicker and narrower than usual; 10. Shoe with crests or points downwards towards the road surface on the toe and quarter, and barbettes or cut away heels; 11. Shoe with calkins doubled over and fitted with rings; 12. Shoe with the upper part of the shoe, i.e., that next to the hoof, turned inwards and bevelled upwards at the heel; 13. Shoe with two calkins; 14. Bar-shoe; 15. Jointed shoe, made to fit any sized hoof; 16. Jointed shoe for use without nails – the shoe is secured by the high border and the heel screw, probably for use in emergencies; 17. Extended hind shoe with calkins; 18. Shoe with one branch thickened into a bevelled calkin at heel; 19. Hind shoe with toe-clip; 20. Hind shoe with extended toe-clip – possibly a veterinary shoe.

Beautiful example of a very late keyhole shoe with rim-fullered groove and heavy calkins, possibly early nineteenth century.

KEYHOLE AND TONGUE SHOES

Although great changes in the state of the roads had taken place in the years following the important Highways Act of 1555 when attempts to regularise the repair of the roads were started, the conditions in some areas were still little better than dirt tracks in the eighteenth century. This was not only due to their use by horses and carriages, waggons and packhorses; between 1776 and 1785 Smithfield market received by road 992,040 beef cattle and 6,859,990 sheep, and these were far from being the majority of cattle, sheep, pigs, geese and turkeys which found their way on to the roads during the period.

Shoes of an archaic type were still made by the more conservative blacksmiths, but seen from a wider viewpoint many changes occurred during the period between 1600 and 1800.

Associated with a mid seventeenth-century smithy at Gloucester, known as Prince Rupert's Smithy, is a group of shoes leading up to the keyhole type. The shoes, varying in size from $4\frac{7}{8}$ by $4\frac{3}{4}$ inches to $5\frac{7}{8}$ by $5\frac{3}{4}$ inches are provided with six nail-holes. In each instance, the shoe has a much rounder external plan, its internal shape leading to chamfered heels and framing

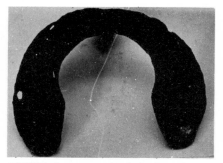

ABOVE: *Large open keyhole shoe of seventeenth century with eight holes (5½ by 5¾ inches, 10 oz).*

TOP LEFT: *Early-type keyhole shoe, c. 1550, only four holes apparent, calkins on each branch, roughly made (4½ by 4⅜ inches, 6 oz).*

CENTRE LEFT: *Keyhole shoe, seventeenth century (c. 1680), with eight holes in a fullered groove (5¼ by 5⅛ inches, 13 oz).*

BOTTOM LEFT: *Well-formed keyhole shoe, seventeenth century, slightly fullered (5⅞ by 6 inches, 19 oz).*

a familiar keyhole pattern. These shoes are probably *c.* 1640–50; they are slightly convex on their under-surfaces and concave on the upper surfaces; some examples have no calkins.

The keyhole group is distinctly larger and heavier in weight than previous types; shoes average 13–14 ounces in weight, while those of the Guildhall type average 10 ounces and those of the wavy-rim variety weigh 5–6 ounces.

The number of nail-holes becomes greater with the heavier shoe, and four or five nail-holes in each branch is quite normal. Nail-holes are frequently spaced all around the shoe and often amounted to as many as twenty by the end of the eighteenth century. This enabled the smith to add more nails when the heavy shoes became loose, thereby increasing the bond. Calkins are present in some cases, but not the heavy calkins on the later Guildhall shoes – often they are just a simple down-turning of the heel.

18

Seventeenth-century keyhole shoes: (left) c. 1650, 4¾ by 4¾ inches, 7 oz; (centre) c. 1700, 5¼ by 5 inches, 10 oz; (right) Prince Rupert Smithy type, 4¾ by 4⅞ inches, 7 oz.

An important feature of this group, besides the obvious keyhole centre hole, is the concave foot surface mentioned above.

These shoes were usually fullered, a method by which a deep groove was introduced on each branch in which the nail-holes were punched. Some later shoes were made from previously fullered iron strip, so that the finished article had an unbroken groove running along the length of the shoe. Where this is not the case but two fullered grooves are present, these are cut into the ground surface by a fullering iron. This fuller allows the heads of the nails to be slightly countersunk below the surface of the shoe

At one time R. M. Murray believed that fullered shoes existed in Europe in Roman times and that they came to England in the thirteenth century, but he later comments that fullering 'does not appear to have been generally adopted in England before the mid sixteenth century'. Gordon Ward goes so far as to suggest that from the evidence of shoes of a known date, there is no sign of fullering before the seventeenth century.

The development of the shoe from the 'Prince Rupert Smithy' type proceeds by way of a shoe of 1706, one possibly of a type used by the cavalry of the Duke of Marlborough. It is fullered, has five nail-holes on each branch and reaches the amazing weight of 44 ounces. Gordon Ward, who examined it, believes it typifies shoes in use at that period but suggests that it may, at that weight, have been a specimen or ceremonial shoe; but bearing in mind the weight of the shoes used

Three shoes showing transition from late seventeenth- to early nineteenth-century shoes: (left) late eighteenth-century, 5⅜ by 5 inches, completely fullered with eleven nail-holes, convex surface to ground, concave surface to foot, 19 oz; (centre) shoe in use in 1775 illustrated by J. Clark, 5⅝ by 5½ inches, 22 oz; (right) modern-looking shoe recommended by J. Clark in 1775, not popular with blacksmiths, but came into use c. 1825, 4½ by 3⅞ inches, 5¾ oz (a riding shoe).

by draught horses in the nineteenth century this may not be the case.

An example of further development along these lines is included in *Observations on the shoeing of horses,* published in 1775 and written by J. Clark. A keyhole shoe is shown with the heels almost touching and its branches are very wide. The type was severely criticised by Clark, who writes: 'the shoes are generally of immoderate weight and length, and every means is used to prevent the frog from resting on the ground, by making the shoe-heels thick, broad and strong, or raising cramps or cankers on them.' He recommends a much lighter shoe, one which in our eyes has a more modern appearance, but he found that 'so much are farriers and grooms prejudiced in favour of the common method of shoeing and paring the feet, that it is with difficulty they can be prevailed upon to make a proper trial of it'.

The tongue shoe was partly contemporary with the keyhole and was probably used more for the riding horse than the draught horse. It was still in use many years after the keyhole pattern had been superseded. Early examples have been dated as late sixteenth-century, but their introduction was more likely at the time of the keyhole shoe of 1700. The difference between the two types lay in the shape of the inner rim. In the case of the tongue shoe, each branch is straight and the heels are well apart, enclosing the shape of a tongue or U-shaped tunnel. In weight they vary between 6 and 14 ounces (with exceptions up to 19 ounces) and have four to five nail-holes in each branch.

With the tongue shoe, the calkins, when present, are abruptly tapered to a width narrower than the branch itself and turned under, while in the later shoes of the type, the heel-ends are square-cut in a manner similar to the early nineteenth-century Regency shoe.

Characteristics of the keyhole shoe (c. 1650–1800)

1. The keyhole-shaped internal edge, which occurred when chamfered heel-ends were brought closer together.
2. Shoes of the middle period are fullered, a feature which on early shoes only extends between the extreme nail-holes in each branch; on shoes dating from 1700 the groove is continuous around the shoe.
3. Nail-holes, increased to four in each branch, by 1700 may number ten per shoe. By the end of the eighteenth century, up to twenty holes may be found evenly spaced in a groove all around the shoe.
4. The nails used were square in section with T-shaped heads, but spiked nails were driven in later shoes.
5. The shoes have a concave surface next to the foot and a convex surface on the underside.
6. Size varies from $4\frac{7}{8}$ by $4\frac{1}{4}$ inches to $5\frac{7}{8}$ by $5\frac{3}{4}$ inches. Weights vary between 10 and 40 ounces.
7. The calkins were made by turning the heels slightly down. Heavy shoes often exhibit a square-cut heel plan.
8. The keyhole shoe was used chiefly on draught horses.
9. Period of use from the early seventeenth century to the late eighteenth century.

Characteristics of tongue-type shoes (c. 1700–1815)

1. Tongue (or 'U' tunnel-like) shape of inner edge plan.
2. Later examples are fullered.
3. Nails numbered eight per shoe with nine or ten in heavier examples.
4. Calkins are tapered and turned under.
5. Heels are wide apart.
6. Size: riding shoe $4\frac{1}{4}$ by $4\frac{1}{2}$ inches, draught shoe 5 by $4\frac{3}{4}$ inches. Weight 6–14 ounces (some heavier draught shoes, 19 ounces).
7. They cover the period between the late seventeenth century and the early nineteenth century.

TOP LEFT: *Very heavy tongue horseshoe, made for a strong draught horse, using ten nail-holes because of its weight, c. 1680-1700 (6½ by 5¾ inches, 21 oz).*

TOP RIGHT: *Lightly fullered tongue shoe with nine holes and calkin on one branch, c. 1750-1820 (5¾ by 5½ inches, 20 oz).*

CENTRE LEFT: *Tongue horseshoe with one calkin and eight well-defined square nail-holes inset within square-sectioned punch-holes, c. 1675 (6 by 5⅛ inches, 11 oz).*

CENTRE RIGHT: *Well-preserved draught-horse tongue shoe with continuous holes, c. 1725 (6 by 5⅝ oz).*

BOTTOM RIGHT: *Tongue shoe with seven holes, for draught horse, c. 1700, not fullered (7 by 6¼ inches, 23 oz).*

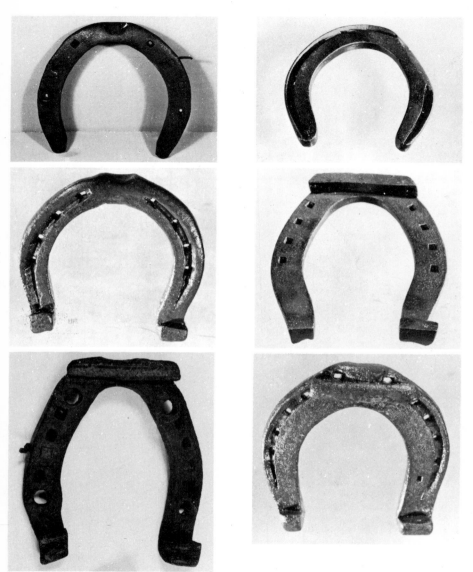

TOP LEFT: *Mid nineteenth-century toe-clip shoe, unfullered, no calkins, standard type.*
TOP RIGHT: *Rim-fullered modern horseshoe showing the heavy wear on one side.*
CENTRE LEFT: *Late nineteenth-century toe-clip saddle-horse shoe with calkins, hand fullered with eight holes (12 oz).* CENTRE RIGHT: *Heavy cast bar toe-clip shoe with calkins, not fullered, late nineteenth century.* BOTTOM LEFT: *Bar toe-clip horseshoe for draught horse, standard type with calkins and large screw-holes for studs at front and heel of shoe, c. 1870–1930 (35 oz.).* BOTTOM RIGHT: *Bar toe-clip shoe with calkins, c. 1900, rim-fullered with two extra nail-holes at toe beyond the bar.*

Stamped shoe, c. 1920, with calkins, unfullered (5½ by 5⅛ inches, 15 oz).

TOE-CLIP AND RIM SHOES

The tongue shoe had gradually modified its shape by the end of the eighteenth century, with the straight branches becoming curved, and by 1820 Joseph Goodwin, who was veterinary surgeon to George IV, wrote that the 'ordinary shoe of most forges is a flat piece of iron, bent to the form of the foot, but often differing in width and length, frequently much longer than the heels and often much shorter. The wearing surface has a groove or fuller all round the outer edge, in which there are usually four holes on each side, and these are kept to the outer rim of the shoe

as near as the shoe will admit. The holes are punched near together, leaving a space at the toe, and also a considerable distance between the last nail and the termination of the shoe. The shoe on the ground-side is convex so that the inner rim, when the foot is on the ground, is the lowest part; from which to the outer edge it describes an inclined plane. Though the form of shoe is more frequently met with than any other, yet there are some forges which make the wearing surface flat.'

In this use of the inclined surface, the shoes in use are following the example set a century before with the keyhole shoe.

The feature which will more easily distinguish the shoe of the early nineteenth century (the Regency type of Gordon Ward) is the use of the toe-clip on the upper surface of the shoe to support the hoof. This innovation takes us back to the plate-shoes of the hippo-sandals, but, except for occasional references in archaeological reports, the toe-clip is believed to have come into fashion with draught horses in the early 1800s and a little later with riding horses. The actual date can be narrowed down to *c.* 1825–30, as Major A. T. Fisher states it was introduced by H. Hallen, who qualified in 1821. William Youatt, writing in 1831, feels that 'clips are necessary on the shoes of all heavy horses', while Sir F. Fitzwygram recommended in 1861 that the whole front of the shoe be turned up (a feature known as the bar-clip). This practice was reintroduced during the First World War.

The use of clips extends to all types of horseshoes, with the possible exception of the racing plate. George Fleming recommended that carriage and saddle horses should have a clip at the toe and that hunting horses needed one on each hind-foot shoe. He also noted that the massive draught horse required, in addition to the toe-clip, toe and heel projections on the ground surface (known as studs or calks) to economise its locomotive power. The use of the great Shire horses during the nineteenth century kept up the demand for the large shoes of the earlier period. These shoes, which Gordon Ward refers to as 'Wood Street type', were of weights ranging from 25 to 46 ounces and in the nineteenth century examples could have up to eighteen nail-holes. Such a shoe, but with a bar toe-clip, was in use in the Hull Docks in the 1930s, and one used by horses of the London Midland & Scottish Railway in 1929 measured $8\frac{1}{2}$ by $8\frac{1}{4}$ inches and weighed 40 ounces. This type of bar toe-clip shoe had a group of four to five holes on each side with additional toe and heel nail-holes.

For ordinary saddle or hunter shoes, the mid nineteenth century was a period of experimentation. The shoe had begun to get lighter, and George Fleming, who was on the council of the Royal College of Veterinary Surgeons, had pronounced that 'we have a perfect right to insist that not a grain of iron more than is absolutely necessary to protect the crust from undue wear, or serve in useful purposes, be applied to the foot'. He also felt that fullering the shoe was unnecessary and introduced by 1864 the stamped-out square-sectioned nail that fitted into a hole in the shoe that was wide at the top and tapered to the bottom. This use of the stamped-out hole was adopted within the trade, but the fullered shoe has continued to the present day.

On the American scene, a shoe was introduced by a Mr Goodenough which received a mixed reception in England. It was made with a flat upper surface following the outline of the hoof, and its under-surface was made concave by having a narrow flat wall circling the outer rim. This iron rim or wall was cut

Three early nineteenth-century shoes introduced by Mr Gray of Sheffield, made of grooved steel cut into a series of ridges and teeth.

HAND-MADE HORSE SHOES.

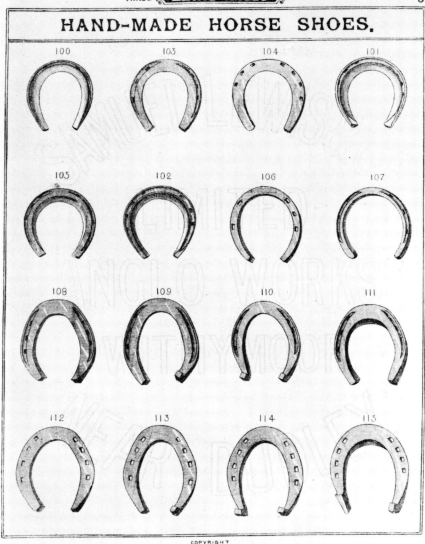

COPYRIGHT

Samuel Lewis catalogue, c. 1920: (top row) riding-horse shoes, 100, 103, 101 fullered, 104 stamped nail-holes; (second row) lightweight shoes, 105, 102, 107 fullered, 106 stamped (106 and 107 possibly racing plates); (third row) 108, 109, 110, 111 fullered shoes with calkins or thickened branches: (bottom row) 112, 113, 114, 115 all stamped shoes.

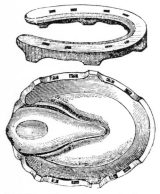

LEFT: *Two views of the patent shoe invented by Mr Goodenough in the USA in 1860. This has built-in calks.* RIGHT: *Patent shoe, made of rubber and metal, c. 1920, on display at Castle Farm Folk Museum, Marshfield, Chippenham.*

away to leave a centre toe-calk and two smaller calks on the quarters. The nail-holes were bored and countersunk, so that the nail-heads could be driven flush.

Another patent, published for John Fowler of Leeds in 1864, was introduced to obviate the injury to horses from the jar transmitted to the hoofs and legs when travelling on hard roads. The preamble notes that 'it is common to put leather between the hoof and the shoe . . . I place the vulcanised india-rubber between two metal shoes; the inner one is nailed to the hoof as hith-erto, and it has studs upon it which pass through the vulcanised india-rubber and so keep it in place'. A novel method for preventing the horse from slipping in mud or on the smooth pavements was introduced by a Mr Gray of Sheffield in the mid nineteenth century. He made shoes of grooved and ridged steel bars which were adapted to secure a firm foothold.

The riding shoe of the time, certainly by the First World War, was almost standardised in weight and size, and it is only in design that any fundamental differences are apparent. Of course in certain special instances, such as the racehorse shoe, there were continuing developments. Racehorses have their normal shoes removed and special aluminium plates fitted for the actual race.

Such plates are designed to reduce suction on wet ground. A shoe current in the 1930s had extra holes at the heels to allow the normal seven nails (four outside and three inside) to be increased or placed in different positions. The flat shoe was generally used for flat racing, but for hurdling or steeplechasing calking might be added at the heel and side-clips at the quarters.

Characteristics of the toe-clip and rim shoe of the nineteenth and twentieth centuries.
Draught shoe
1. The tongue-type shoe continued to be used, gradually taking a rounder shape towards the middle of the nineteenth century, although still remaining flat and broad.
2. Toe-clips were introduced 1825–30, and the bar toe-clip was used on heavier shoes 1880–1930. Side-clips were also used from the 1840s.
3. Draught shoes were frequently un-fullered.
4. Concave upper surfaces and convex lower surfaces are normal characteristics.
5. Nails increased; there may be up to eighteen or twenty holes all round the shoe, but not all these were in use at the same time. Nails were usually No. 12 (3 inches long).
6. The tongue-type shoes changed to

the rim-type and between 1890 and 1930 the bar toe-clip shoe was common.
7. Size: increases from 5⅞ by 4 inches up to 8¾ by 8½ inches; current twentieth-century shoes are 6 by 5¾ inches. Weight: 25–40 ounces; modern shoes 19–23 ounces.

Riding shoe
1. Its shape is a continuation of the Dove shoe; it becomes a true rim-type shoe made from a narrow band of iron.
2. Toe-clips with fore shoe and side-clips with the hind shoes were used.

3. If the shoe is fullered all round, it was probably made from factory-fullered bar in most cases. When it is fullered for the length of the nail-holes, it was probably hand-fullered.
4. Nail-holes were punched counter-sunk; they number from five to eight with usually four holes outside and three inside. Size No. 6 (2⅛ inches long) nail was used for hunters, and size No. 3 (1¾ inches long) for racehorses.
5. Size: 5½ by 4¾ inches up to 6 by 5¾ inches. Weight: 9–14 ounces.

RIGHT: *Two deeply fullered lightweight racing shoes, made of aluminium, early twentieth century.*
BELOW: *Late nineteenth century shoe with deeply fullered groove on each branch with pointed toe shape, a specialised pattern.*
BOTTOM: *Lightweight racing shoe, deeply fullered on one branch, with the other branch not nailed, c. 1900 (4 by 4½ inches, 5¼ oz).*
BOTTOM RIGHT: *Display of shoes at Castle Farm Folk Museum, Marshfield, Chippenham: one row has three donkey-shoes and a miniature shoe.*

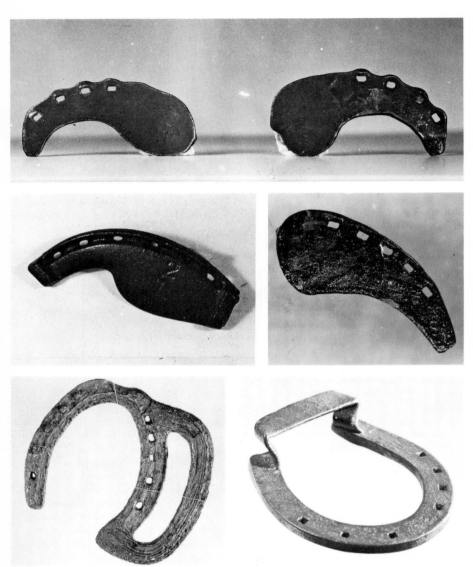

TOP: *Pair of ox-shoes with wavy-rimmed edges (Aylesbury Museum).* CENTRE LEFT: *American cast ox-shoe from West Virginia, USA, with heavily fullered groove and calkins.* CENTRE RIGHT: *Part of ox-shoe with even rim and no calkin.* BOTTOM LEFT: *Veterinary shoe with ten holes and extended bracket to offer balance, early nineteenth century.* BOTTOM RIGHT: *Veterinary shoe with heel bar, seven nail-holes, c. 1900.*

A pair of lawn-shoes – overshoes made of leather with sewn leather soles and two straps on each shoe to fit it to the hoof of the pony or horse, used for pulling a mowing machine (early twentieth century).

OX, MULE, DONKEY AND SPECIAL SHOES

The ox was one of the earliest animals to be used for agricultural purposes in western Europe, this first occurring in the neolithic period, while in Egypt it could have been as early as 3,500 BC. Among ancient writers Columella describes a sandal of broom or wickerwork for use on lame oxen, but in England the earliest reference is probably that, dating from the eleventh century, when Guibert de Nugent mentions rustics who shod their oxen like horses.

This must have been a reference to the use of two separate plates on each foot, as the foot of the ox is bifurcated, so that one was needed for the outer margins of each claw. Ox-shoes seldom survive to the same degree as horseshoes because they are made of relatively thinner material than a horseshoe and this rusts through much more quickly. The resultant fragments tend to look more like broken sections of horseshoes.

Metal ox-shoes have been replaced in some areas of the Far East by rubber cut from old motor tyres, which, being flexible, will 'give' to the motion of the ox's foot. The ox-shoe, like the horseshoe, has several types which varied in shape from a plain bent piece of strip iron to an elaborately shell-shaped crescent with a clip.

Mule and donkey-shoes can usually be distinguished from each other by the frequently pointed heels of the mule-shoe, so that it resembles a large metal staple. It is possible that many have ended up in gateposts acting as gate catches after they served their primary purpose. The donkey-shoe tends to be similar to the horseshoe, but is smaller, lighter (7–12 ounces) and longer in relation to its width, similar to a schoolboy's large magnet. In the nineteenth century regular weekly markets were held at Islington at which many of the three thousand donkeys imported annually to Britain were sold. Many came from Ireland and were driven from the coast to London in droves of about one hundred. They were heavily shod in Ireland, but after the long walk they would often be re-shod in London with a rather lighter shoe.

The pony-shoe is quite round in shape, often small and light in weight (5–7½ ounces). The worn-out shoes can often be mistaken for iron heel-plates from the heavy boots of working men.

Whenever there is a variation in shoe style which appears to be out of period or out of character, it is almost invariably labelled by collectors as a 'pathological', 'surgical' or 'veterinary' shoe. Whether the many varieties so termed are accurately designated is a moot point, but it is true that a number of unusual shoes have been introduced to correct a fault or ease an injury. These shoes are often larger than usual and frequently have a characteristic bar across the heel. In some cases one of the branches may be considerably wider than the other, or the branches merge into one plate. It is always possible that the hipposandal was a Roman surgical shoe; it was certainly heavy, but no heavier than many of the shoes made to be used by the nineteenth-century draught horses. One of the more familiar problems with horses is 'brushing', in which the fetlock of the opposite leg is injured through being struck by the shoe of the hind foot. To counteract this tendency, an anti-brushing shoe was devised which has a fullered and calked outer branch and an un-fullered, 'knocked-up' inner branch with a wedge heel. This knocked-up shoe has no nails in the inner branch except for one near to the toe. Another problem is 'overreaching', in which the horse strikes and injures the heel of the forefoot with the hind foot, often bringing the latter alongside the forefoot. The shoe designed to correct this fault, known as the 'anti-overreach shoe', has the back edge of the toe of the hind shoe rounded to reduce its cutting edge

and it is also set well back on the hoof, after having a part of the toe rasped away.

Other surgical shoes include the Fitzwygram shoe, triangular in section with the toe turned upwards with a sharp edge. This was designed by General Sir P. F. Fitzwygram to correct stumbling. A similar shoe, introduced by Major General Sir L. J. Blenkinsop, is somewhat wider and made of thinner plate. On the fore shoe the front half of the toe is bent upwards and the hind shoe is supplied with two toe-clips; it could be 6¾ by 6 inches and weigh 23 ounces. In many cases the farmer or horse-owner could not afford to shoe his horse with custom-made surgical shoes, even if he knew that they existed; instead a leather boot tied around the ankle of the afflicted foot sufficed. Indeed, a good wrapping of sacking or hessian frequently eased the injury.

Other types of shoes were made for special uses, such as the 'lawn' shoe used by ponies and small horses when pulling a lawn-mower, so that their hoofs would not damage the turf. In very sharp wintry weather it was the custom to remove two or three nails from each shoe and replace them with 'frosty' nails. These protruded below the surface and helped to prevent slipping on icy ground. A special shoe was also made with two holes drilled having a screw thread, and in frosty weather special studs or calks could be screwed in. The advantage of the screw-in studs was their longer life during a period of wintry weather, as the frost nails tended to wear down rather quickly. Catalogues show a number of stud designs and one may infer that considerable personal preferences had to be taken into account by the manufacturers.

Metals other than iron were used in certain cases in the production of shoes. Copper shoes were necessary for the horses employed for transport within the gunpowder works in the Lake District and were in use until the closure of the works in the 1920s and 1930s. Brass shoes are also known to have been made.

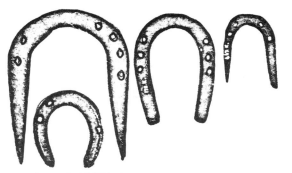

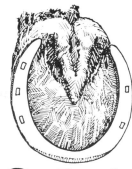

TOP LEFT: *Large mule-shoe (22 oz), pony-shoe within, c. 1920; donkey-shoe (7 oz); donkey-shoe (3½ oz) (drawings from items in Hull Museum Collection).*

TOP RIGHT: *Fitwygram shoe, made to overcome stumbling with the toe slightly turned up and a flat narrow shoe.*

ABOVE: *Items from the Samuel Lewis catalogue, c. 1920: steel frost screws, cogs, etc, for use in bad weather.*

ABOVE LEFT: *Mud shoe, made of a wooden patten supported below by two metal bars. The shoe is fixed to the hoof by means of the shaped metal clips and tightened with a wing-nut.*

LEFT: *Stamped shoe, with eight holes and adjustable frog support. This hinged plate may be raised or removed as necessary; late nineteenth century.*

BOTTOM LEFT: *Veterinary horseshoe, fullered with frog support, c. 1865.*

BOTTOM RIGHT: *Metal overshoe, used in bad weather. This has a rim into which the horseshoe fits and the heel-bar is then tightened with the nut to secure it.*

FOLKLORE AND HORSESHOE COLLECTIONS

Strange stories and superstitions are linked with horseshoes. This is due in part to their resemblance to lunar symbols, i.e. the horned new moon. Finding a horseshoe and nailing it over a door was believed to keep away witches, and in the old days nailing a horseshoe to a suspected witch's door was thought to be a way of keeping her in.

Finding a horseshoe in the road is believed to bring good luck. This was certainly believed in Amsterdam around 1687, while the use of horseshoes or silvered cardboard copies at weddings is commonplace today and calculated to ensure a happy marriage. When the shoe is nailed over a door, or on a barn, there is doubt in some people's minds as to the way it should be fixed. One school of thought would nail it upright with the heels in the air, as this keeps the 'luck' in, while others nail them downwards and take the chance that it will not run out. So while people kept the odd horseshoe around the house or farm, and often nailed it up for luck, the collecting of shoes, with a critical eye as to types and historical period, does not go back much earlier than the beginning of the twentieth century. The collections of Gordon Ward and R. M. Murray, both writers on the history of horseshoes, have been mentioned; that of Gordon Ward formed the basis of the display at the City of Hull Museum. Nowadays most folk and craft museums have a collection, often related to a farrier's or smith's workshop on exhibition, and George Flinders, blacksmith at Scarrington, Notts, is one of several smiths who have built large columns of horseshoes reaching a height of twenty feet. Another is at the smithy at Great Brickhill, Bucks.

But perhaps the most remarkable collection of horseshoes is that at Oakham Castle in Leicestershire (formerly Rutland). When the estate was given by William the Conqueror to Henry de Ferrers, who became an inspector of farriers, he was also granted the right to demand a horseshoe from every peer of the realm who visited the manor. The edict of Henry II records: 'The first time a peer of the realm come within the precinct of the Manor of Oakham, he forfeits a shoe from his horse to be nailed to the castle gate and should he refuse it, or a compensation in money, the bailiff is entitled to take it by force.' So a fine collection of shoes has been built up and as the castle is now open to the public, they may be seen in all their glory. The shoes, which vary from ones of normal size to monstrosities almost two feet across, are painted and surmounted with coronets and carry the names of the donors. The earliest is dated 1600 and was presented by Edward, Lord Dudley. Since that time a collection numbering over two hundred specimens has been built up. Many of these were specially made, although several of the older ones may well have been taken from horses at the gate. Shoes following that given by Charles William Francis, Earl of Gainsborough, in 1882 were often made of cast iron, as this material enabled the donor to include his crest as an integral part of the design. In 1893 the horseshoes were cast in iron with raised letters, and the twentieth-century shoes were made by S. R. Russell & Sons Ltd. More recent shoes, from 1945–70, were made by an Oakham blacksmith. Many famous names are included in the collection, with fine examples presented by the Prince Regent in 1814 and more recently Prince Philip, Duke of Edinburgh, in 1957 (see page 2).

As well as being kept for luck, collected or used for decorative purposes, horseshoes have also been used in sport. Horseshoe throwing is traditionally played in East Anglia, and the game is believed to be as old as horse ploughing itself. The rules are similar to quoits, and there are no restrictions as to the weight, size or type of horseshoe used, or the length of the pitch. It is a game to be set up in minutes and played with any handy shoe.